THE
AWAKENED
BEING

Living with Clarity, Purpose,
and Divine Insight

GWEN R. ROBERTS

DEDICATION

For the Seekers who want a better understanding of themselves and their place in the universe. May these pages light a spark within you, helping you on your path to awakening.

To the Skeptics who approach life with a questioning mind, which is a valuable asset. May these words challenge your preconceived notions and open your heart to the prospect of a life full of clarity, purpose, and divine insight.

To the Awakened Beings who are on a path of conscious awareness. May this book serve as a companion, providing reflections and insights to help you in your journey to living a life filled with purpose and divine connection.

ACKNOWLEDGEMENT

I am deeply grateful to the following people without whom this book wouldn't be possible:

My teachers, mentors, and spiritual leaders, for guiding me along the path of awakening. Your wisdom, kindness, and undying confidence in the human spirit have served as my guiding stars.

My family and friends for making it possible for this book to be created. Your constant love, understanding, and (sometimes forced) patience helped me through periods of doubt and writer's block.

My editor, Suzanne Smith, whose keen eye and precise touch guided the flow of thoughts.

WHY THIS BOOK?

The pages of "The Awakened Being" contain a map, not to a specific location but to the vast landscape of your own awakened potential. This book is your companion, providing simplified and broken down tools and inspiration to help you live with clarity, purpose, and divine insight.

Imagine a life in which the fog of confusion is lifted, replaced by a clear understanding of your authentic self and your place in the world. "The Awakened Being" provides you with practical methods for quieting the mental chatter and cultivating inner peace, allowing you to see yourself and your environment with newfound understanding.

You'll learn to hone your intuition—those subtle whispers that lead you to decisions that align with your deepest purpose. This book offers frameworks for identifying your core values and desires, paving the way for a life that seems not simply busy but actually meaningful.

TABLE OF CONTENTS

INTRODUCTION

Have you ever found yourself lost in a Sunday afternoon social media scroll, surrounded by images of flawless lives and feeling as though yours is missing something? Alternatively, it could be the other way around: even though you're gazing at an incredible mountain range that makes you gasp, a dull ache is pressing against your chest. Whether you're climbing a mountain peak or sitting on your couch, loneliness can still seep in.

That uneasy feeling that lurks at the periphery of our lives is something we've all experienced. It takes on a million forms, including persistent job discontent, a need for closer relationships, and a void that is unsatisfied by new technology or fashionable clothing. We seek out transient joys and divert our attention, but the emptiness never goes away.

This desire is the call to awakening, my friend. It's a subdued nudge toward a more meaningful life—one in which connection and purpose are more than simply catchphrases from motivational speeches you've read online.

An Awakened Being is not some fantastical being that is always happy. It's someone who has paid attention to that persistent feeling within and has decided to push past the void and begin to go farther. They've found their inner compass—that still, quiet voice that points them in the direction of a life that feels authentic rather than a glossy, magazine-perfect ideal. They've discovered the inner spark—the link to something more than their daily to-do list. This flame ignites a desire to connect with the invisible forces that influence our reality and to unravel the secrets of life.

An Awakened Being does not go through life unaffected by difficulties. They have uncertainties, anxieties, and days when it seems too black to bear. However, they have developed an inner clarity and quiet strength that enable them to weather these storms with grace. They have faith in a greater purpose that is being carried out, even when they are unable to perceive it. They see existence as a collaboration between our will and the ever-shifting universe.

The call to awakening within you is presented in this book, "The Awakened Being: Living with Clarity, Purpose, and Divine Insight." It's not a set of rules, but guidance. We'll explore the fundamentals of woke life, including useful tools, exercises, and honest, no-BS conversation. You'll discover how to still your thoughts and access your intuition's insight. We'll look at how to communicate with the divine presence that permeates everything that exists.

This will not be an easy journey. It calls for self-reflection, self-control, and a readiness to confront the possibly soiled aspects of oneself. However, the benefits are substantial. You'll develop an inner calm that endures the unavoidable setbacks of life. You'll discover a source of inspiration and direction that will guide you to a life that genuinely fulfills you. You will become aware of how everything is interrelated and feel a deep sense of belonging to something greater than yourself.

Are you prepared to take the call? Now let's get started.

PART I

FOUNDATIONS OF

AWAKENED LIVING

CHAPTER 1

AWAKENING YOUR INNER COMPASS

Have you ever had the feeling that you are a ship at sea, blown around by the storms and currents, not knowing where you are going? In our fast-paced, information-rich world, feeling disoriented and insecured is a typical experience. Every day, we are overwhelmed with external stimuli such as social media feeds, views from others, and society's expectations. We lose touch with the still, inner voice that is our true selves because we grow so used to the noise of the outside world. Your compass, or inner voice, is what directs you toward a purposeful and fulfilled existence.

Developing an inner sense of direction is essential to being an Awakened Being. It's about revealing your true self by removing the layers of self-doubt and indoctrination. It's about taking off the masks we put on for the outside world and finding the colorful, distinct person behind them. Your deepest goals, your gifts, and the driving force that will lead you to a life of authenticity and contribution are all included in your essence.

However, how do we start this self-examination? How can we tune into the whispers of our inner compass and block out the outside noise? This is where self-awareness practices are useful. A useful tool is keeping a journal. Select a peaceful area, grab a pen and paper, and just begin writing. Perfect language and creating a masterpiece are not important; this is a discussion that you and you alone are having.

Write about your disappointments, worries, and dreams. Write about the things that make you happy, what ignites your soul, and what makes you feel fully alive. As you write, you could notice reoccurring themes and patterns that hint at your basic desires and ideals. Take note of these themes without passing judgment; they are hints that will help you find your true self again.

Meditation is another powerful method for developing self-awareness. Close your eyes, find a comfortable position, and concentrate on your breathing. Observe your chest's rise and fall, as well as the coolness of the air as it enters your nose. Remind yourself to pay attention to your breathing when your thoughts stray—which they will!—but do so kindly and without passing judgment. The goal of meditation is to develop the ability to notice your thoughts and emotions without letting them consume you, not to reach a state of absolute emptiness. When you practice meditation regularly, it creates a bridge to inner stillness, a place where you can communicate with your inner wisdom, the still, silent voice inside of you.

Let's now discuss intention-setting. This has nothing to do with bending the cosmos to your will. It's about becoming a conscious participant in your own journey and bringing yourself into alignment with life's flow. You sow a seed in your subconscious mind when you make an intention. This seed attracts opportunities and experiences that align with your desires like a beacon.

Here's a quick tip for creating intentions: Choose a peaceful area and close your eyes. Breathe deeply for a few moments. Ask yourself, "What do I actually seek in this moment?" may be the confidence to follow a creative passion or greater clarity on your life path. After you've determined what you want, put it into a succinct and understandable phrase. Say to yourself silently, "I intend to discover my life's mission with clarity and joy," for instance. Feel the energy of your intention flowing through you as you repeat this.

This is where it becomes real. How can you put these fresh, self-aware realizations into practice? This is where personal mission statements and fundamental beliefs come into play. Your life is guided by the essential principles that comprise your core values. These are the things that are deeply important to you and are not negotiable. Maybe it's generosity, ingenuity, or serving others. Making judgments based on your true self rather than outside forces is easier when you are aware of your basic principles.

It's time to create a personal mission statement after you have a clear understanding of your basic beliefs. This is a strong statement that captures your goals and purpose; it's not a dry piece of corporate document. It ought to be succinct, motivational, and wholly original. "I am a passionate champion for social justice, inspired by a desire to build a more equal world for all," is one example of what I mean.

Recall that your statement of personal mission is an ongoing process. It may change as you go through life and gain new insights. Having a guiding principle or North Star to guide you through life's inevitable twists and turns is crucial.

It takes time to find your inner compass. It involves developing an inquisitive mindset and a readiness to delve into the core of your being. Your inner compass will become more visible as you peel away the layers of cultural conditioning and self-doubt, pointing you in the direction of a life of honesty, purpose, and divine connection. The key to being an Awakened Being is to live a life that is in harmony with your innermost self and that benefits others as a whole. Recall that the path of self-discovery is a never-ending adventure that is interspersed with quiet reflection intervals and epiphanies. Embrace the process and have faith in your inner guidance and get prepared to be astounded by the Awakened Being that is just waiting to be found within.

Here are some more exercises to help you become more self-aware and build your bond with your inner compass:

- **Spend time in nature**: Being surrounded by nature can help you rediscover your natural sense of belonging and has a profoundly relaxing effect on the psyche. Go for a stroll through the forest, relax by a bubbling creek, or just stare up at the stars. Take in the wonder and unity of all things, and let them motivate you.

- **Develop an attitude of thankfulness**: Take time to recognize and be grateful for all of life's blessings. This will change your outlook and make you feel more content. Every day, list three things for which you are thankful in your gratitude diary. This easy exercise can make a big difference in your general health and ability to connect with your inner knowledge.

- **Engage in creative expression**: Whether it's writing, painting, dancing, or music-making, creative expression enables you to connect with a deeper part of yourself. Give your creativity a free rein, and don't worry about producing a masterpiece. You might uncover untapped abilities and insights along the way that deepen your awareness of who you are.

- **Embrace silence:** Setting aside time for silence can be a radical act of self-care in our always connected world. The mind can calm down, and the inner voice can be heard more clearly in silence. Every day, set aside some time for calm, distraction-free reflection. When it comes to cultivating inner calm and self-awareness, this exercise can be surprisingly effective.

Be patient with yourself as you go out on this path to discover your inner compass. There will be obstacles and periods of uncertainty. That is entirely typical. It's important to keep going, to keep investigating, and to keep believing in your inner voice. Your ability to negotiate life's problems with greater grace and purpose will increase as your inner compass grows clearer. You'll make decisions that are consistent with your basic beliefs and gravitate toward chances that make you happy and fulfilled. This is the way to become an Awakened Being; it's a life where you live true to who you are and share your special talents with the world.

RECONNECTING WITH YOUR TRUE SELF

Everybody gets a bit lost occasionally, buried beneath a mountain of "shoulds" and demands from society. This tames the wild, energetic you—the one that gets excited about the most unlikely things and yearns for life-altering adventures. It's reconnecting with this authentic self that starts the magic.

Here's how to fan the spark:

- **Remember what makes you "you":** What childhood activities did you enjoy doing? What activities make you lose track of time? Even if it seems absurd at first, rekindle those long-forgotten interests.

- **Challenge your routines:** Shake things up! Try a new meal, talk to a complete stranger, or take a different route to work. Venturing beyond your comfort zone might reveal your inner creativity and self-awareness.

- **Embrace the present moment**: Set aside your phone and give your whole attention to your surroundings. Take in the sights, sounds, and nuances; these thoughtful moments can help you rediscover the basic pleasures of life.

CULTIVATING SELF-AWARENESS

Self-awareness can be compared to picking up a weak radio signal. It sounds like a mess of static at first. But you can learn to tune out the background noise and concentrate on the underlying signals with practice. Here are some strategies for amplifying your inner voice:

- **Quiet Observation**: Develop the curiosity to examine your own feelings and ideas. Spend some time each day just observing what's happening inside of you. Do you feel happy, annoyed, or anxious? What caused this feeling to arise? Just watch; don't judge yourself. You'll see patterns that provide hints about your inner landscape and your priorities.

- **Body Language**: A lot of the time, your body speaks louder than words. Take note of your body's feelings. A tense jaw may be a sign of underlying stress, whereas a comfortable stance conveys contentment. Observe how your body responds to various circumstances and individuals. Emotionally hidden truths can be uncovered by these subtle indicators.

- **Curiosity is Key:** Treat yourself with the same level of interest you would an interesting new acquaintance. Which routines do you have? What spurs you on to action? What makes you feel exhausted? Investigate the truthful answers to these questions for yourself. Achieving a flawless state of enlightenment is not the goal of self-awareness; rather, it is about cultivating a cordial inner conversation and being open to hearing your true self.

Gaining self-awareness will enable you to access your inner compass's power. This inner guiding system will assist you in making decisions that are consistent with your basic beliefs, navigating life's obstacles with more clarity, and finally figuring out the route to a happy and genuine existence.

THE POWER OF INTENTION

Say you find yourself standing at a crossroads. There are endless paths in front of you, all pointing in the direction of unknown places. This is the feeling of living without intention. We are tossed around by fate as we walk aimlessly. Setting intentions, however, is similar to raising a sail since it allows you to guide the wind of the universe in the direction you want to go.

The beauty is that intention-setting isn't about making the universe do what you want it to. It's about becoming a conscious participant in your own journey and bringing yourself into alignment with life's flow. You sow a seed in your subconscious mind when you make an intention. This seed attracts opportunities and experiences that align with your desires like a beacon.

So, how are these potent seeds planted?

- **Make a clear decision**: What do you really want right now? Perhaps it's a greater sense of calm in your day-to-day existence, or perhaps it's the bravery to follow a creative passion. Spend some time introspecting and determining your main goal.

- **Create Your Statement:** After you've determined what you want, put it into a succinct and understandable sentence. Say to yourself silently, "I desire to cultivate inner peace with equanimity and grace," for instance. Feel the energy of your intention flowing through you as you repeat this.

- **Have faith in the process:** If outcomes don't show up right away, don't give up. Setting intentions is a journey, not a sprint. You will find yourself getting closer to your chosen destination as you continue to sow these seeds of intention.

ALIGNING WITH YOUR VALUES

Your non-negotiables, the guiding principles that make your heart sing, are your core values. They serve as the compass points that direct you toward a genuine and contented life.

So, how do you recognize these values?

- **Life Audit**: Step back and assess your life, including past decisions, present routines, and happy and frustrating times. What trends show up? What gives you a feeling of direction?
- **Empirical Principles**: Examine those you find admirable. Which traits do they exhibit? It's likely that those attributes align with your own basic principles.
- **The "Hell Yeah" Test**: Imagine receiving a job offer or being given the chance to move. Does it elicit an enthusiastic "yes!" or a hesitant "maybe"? Have faith in your instincts. It may not be in line with your basic beliefs if it doesn't feel like a clear "Hell yeah!"

After you have a firm understanding of your values, it's time to put them into practice. Let them serve as a beacon of wisdom for all of your daily choices, large and small. This is how you authentically and purposefully negotiate the ups and downs of life.

CHAPTER 2

UNVEILING THE DIVINE WITHIN

"The most beautiful thing we may encounter is the mysterious," this is a quote attributed to Albert Einstein. This inherent mystery transcends the material world, encompassing the vast realm of the divine, which is invisible. Humanity has always tried to make contact with this invisible power, which exists outside the bounds of our daily existence.

For the Awakened Being this connection is a living experience, not a distant longing,. It's the realization that the divine is a spark that lives inside each of us rather than an outside force.

However, what exactly is this "divine within"? It has nothing to do with adhering to a specific religion or set of beliefs. Realizing the innate connectivity and fullness of everything is key. It's the realization that we are a part of a huge and amazing network of existence rather than solitary entities.

This relationship with the divine takes many forms. When considering the natural world, some people experience awe and amazement. Awe-inspiring sights like the expanse of the universe, the delicate balance of an ecosystem, and the intricate movement of galaxies evoke a sense of being a part of something greater than ourselves.

For others, the divine speaks via deeds of kindness and generosity. A more peaceful society can be created by doing good deeds like lending a sympathetic ear to a friend, volunteering for a cause you believe in, or helping a complete stranger. In these instances, we become channels for the divine, physically expressing compassion and love.

Deeply still times can also be used to encounter the divine inside. A heightened awareness appears in the still moment between ideas. We establish a connection with a source of calm and harmony that surpasses the day-to-day turmoil of existence. We can hear the faint guiding of our inner compass, the whispers of intuition, while we are in this state of inner calm.

Here's the key: the divine within isn't something to be achieved; it's something to be unveiled. Under a veil of fear, indoctrination, and self-doubt, there is already a dazzling light. It is our responsibility to develop practices that enable the divine light to peek through these layers and to gradually eradicate them.

Your life changes as you discover the divine inside. You feel more at ease and have a greater sense of purpose. Not only do you grow in empathy and comprehension for other people, but also for yourself. Knowing that life is unfolding for a purpose and that you are a part of a larger picture inspires confidence.

This is not to suggest that there will be sunshine and rainbows in your life. There will still be challenges, but you'll be more resilient and have a stronger sense of inner power to overcome them. You will realize that the divine light shines within you and guides you towards a better tomorrow, even in the midst of darkness.

RECOGNIZING THE DIVINE SPARK IN ALL

Despite their apparent differences, science and spirituality both provide convergent views on the interconnection of all things. Everything in the universe is ultimately formed of tiny vibrating threads of energy, as science shows through the lens of physics. We are all made of the same fundamental substance as the trees and the stars, and we are all in a cosmic symphony.

Spiritually speaking, several faiths refer to a supernatural energy known as the universal life force that permeates all living things. We are connected to the entire universe via this energy, not simply to one another. Understanding this interdependence promotes a profound respect for the chain of life and a sense of connection with all creatures.

der it this way: you are a part of the melody, interacting with the surrounding instruments, rather than just a solitary note in a large orchestra. Every individual contributes in a different way to the magnificent symphony of life.

Discovering the divinity inside involves more than just finding your own inner flame; it also entails seeing the spark present in all living things. Being conscious of this fact reminds us that we are all a part of something greater than ourselves, which cultivates compassion. It forces us to take on the role of guardians of the earth, preserving the fragile balance of life.

The boundaries that separate the "self" from the "other" start to fall away as you develop this sense of interconnection. You feel a strong sense of connection to the natural world, a profound sense of belonging, and a fresh understanding of the divinity that is innate in all living things.

EXPLORING YOUR SPIRITUAL LINEAGE

Though the divine spark whispers in everyone of us, the song varies depending on the culture and tradition. Humanity has long sought a way to connect with the divine, from the meditative practices of Buddhism to the ancient wisdom of Hinduism, and from the Abrahamic traditions of Judaism, Christianity, and Islam to the philosophies of indigenous civilizations.

These customs have strong things in common, even though they appear to be very different from one another:

- **The interconnectedness of all things**: The idea that humans are a part of a huge web of existence rather than something apart from the universe is emphasized in many faiths.
- **Compassion and service**: From the Golden Rule to the Bodhisattva ideal, most traditions

emphasize the value of doing good deeds and serving the greater good.

- **Inner peace and stillness:** The goal of mindfulness exercises, prayer, and meditation is to develop inner serenity and establish a connection with a deeper sense of being.

Even if you don't believe in any particular dogma, exploring various traditions can provide insightful tools and viewpoints for discovering the divine within you. Consider it like a buffet: try out many techniques and determine which ones speak to you.

Accepting the depth of the human experience in its quest for the divine is essential. You will learn from studying these traditions that the way to become aware of the divine within you is ultimately a personal one, a song that only you can sing.

CULTIVATING A DEVOTED HEART

Being devoted isn't about mindlessly adhering to religious doctrine. It involves developing a sense of belonging and a sense that you are a part of something greater than yourself. It's the realization that you possess a divine spark—the same spark that animates everything in the universe.

So, how can we develop this devotion in our day-to-day lives? To help you get started, consider these few exercises:

- **Gratitude Ritual:** Spend some time in silence before going to bed or when you wake up to reflect on the positive aspects of your life. It could be anything, such as a mouthwatering dinner, a comforting buddy, or the sun's warmth on your skin. Allow appreciation to overflow from your heart, creating a bond with the universe's plenty.

- **Acts of Service**: One of the most effective ways to show someone you care is to assist them. Give your time, lend a stranger a helping hand, or carry out a random act of kindness. By performing these deeds of service, you open up a channel for the divine, showing compassion and fostering world peace.

- **Mindful Moments**: Throughout the day, pause to breathe deeply and to simply be in the moment. Take note of the surrounding sights, sounds, and sensations. Sensate the air filling your lungs and the ground beneath your feet. By bringing you back to the present, these mindful moments help you develop awe for the wonder and beauty of life.

Try out these techniques, see what speaks to you, and watch as your sense of spiritual connection expands and deepens. Your life becomes a manifestation of that connection as your devotion grows, radiating kindness, love, and service to others.

THE LANGUAGE OF THE UNIVERSE

Have you ever had an unexpected random thought pop into your head just to have it confirmed moments later by a stranger's conversation, a billboard you see on the way to work, or a song on the radio? This isn't merely a coincidence; rather, it's the universe speaking to you through synchronicities, which is its own distinct language.

Meaningful coincidences, or seemingly random happenings with a deeper link, are called synchronicities. They serve as tiny reminders or nudges from the universe, guiding you in a particular way or bringing up significant issues. Being alert and paying attention is crucial.

Here's how to spot these hints of the divine:

- **Recurring Symbols**: Keep an eye out for any numbers or symbols that keep coming up in your life. It can be a certain tune that appears out of nowhere, a bird you see everywhere, or a series of numbers that continually catch your attention. Spend some time thinking about what these symbols might mean to you because they frequently have personal significance.
- **Intuitive Hits**: There are moments when a seemingly random idea or picture just pops into

your head. Have faith in your instincts. These gut feelings may be signs from the universe pointing you in the direction of a problem-solving opportunity.

- **Conversations that Mirror Your Thoughts**: Have you ever been thinking about anything in particular and then, just moments later, heard someone else bring up the same subject? There is synchronicity here! It can indicate that you're headed in the correct direction or that something you've been thinking about is being confirmed by the cosmos.

Recall that the purpose of synchronicities is not to create links where none exist. It requires a certain level of awareness to hear them because they are faint whispers. Keep a journal and record these incidents. You will eventually begin to recognize patterns and get better at understanding the peculiar language of the world. You'll feel more a part of life's flow and more confident as you become more aware of synchronicities and believe that life is working in your favor.

PART II

CULTIVATING CLARITY AND PURPOSE

CHAPTER 3

QUIETING THE MIND
FOR INNER CLARITY

The human mind is an amazing instrument. It enables us to solve challenging puzzles, think critically, and produce artistic masterpieces. However, there is another side to this issue. Our minds can also be unrelenting chatterboxes that constantly barrage us with worries, anxieties, and thoughts. This mental chatter can be a major hindrance to inner clarity, which makes it challenging to access our creativity, connect with our intuition, and achieve genuine peace of mind.

It is crucial for the Awakened Being to cultivate inner clarity. It serves as the cornerstone around which everything else about awakening is constructed. Stillness of mind allows you to hear the faint guiding of the divine inside, the whispers of your inner compass. You can reach your greatest potential and draw from a creative wellspring.

How then do we still our minds and develop inner clarity? While there isn't a panacea, there are effective techniques that can be useful. Let's explore some of them.

Meditation: The Gateway to Stillness

Meditation is probably the most well-known technique for developing inner clarity. It's about learning to observe your thoughts and feelings without letting them consume you, not about reaching a state of perfect emptiness. Picture yourself relaxing beside a swiftly flowing river. Thoughts pass by like leaves; you see them but don't hold on to them. Meditation develops into a place where the mind calms and inner clarity appears with regular practice.

There are numerous approaches to meditation. Some focus on the breath, others on mantras (repeated sounds or phrases), and still others involve guided visualizations. Try different things and see what speaks to you. Meditating for even a short time each day can have a big impact on your capacity to clear your thoughts and find inner clarity.

The Power of Presence

Quieting the mind is only one aspect of inner clarity; another is being totally present in the moment. We are buried in our thoughts for extended periods of time, either fretting about the future or ruminating on the past. We are unable to fully appreciate the richness of the current moment because of this incessant mental chatter.

Here are some ways to cultivate presence:

- **Mindful Movement:** You can become more anchored in the present moment by engaging in practices like yoga, tai chi, or even mindful strolling. Take note of your body's physical sensations, such as the rise and fall of your breath and the feel of your feet on the ground.

- **Engage Your Senses:** Take the time to taste your meal when you're eating. Allow the noise of the song to envelope you while you listen. Put your phone away and give the entire conversation your full attention while you're with people you love. By engaging your senses, you focus your attention on the present moment.

- **The Power of Nature:** Being in nature is one of the most effective ways to develop presence. Take in the wonder and beauty of the surrounding natural environment. Give up the chatter in your head and just be.

Taming the Inner Critic

The voice of self-doubt, our inner critic, can provide a serious challenge to achieving inner clarity. Negative ideas that tell us we're not worthy, intelligent, or good enough are constantly bombarding us. However, your inner critic is a conditioned aspect of your mind, not who you really are.

Here are a few strategies for quieting your inner critic:

- **Being aware is essential:** Recognizing the voice of your inner critic is the first step. Take note of the judgments and self-deprecating ideas that surface. Instead of criticizing yourself for thinking these thoughts, just observe them objectively.

- **Challenge Negative Beliefs:** Once a negative thought pattern has been recognized, question its veracity. Is it really grounded in truth, or is it just your inner critic trying to hold you back?

- **Self-Compassion is the Antidote:** Show yourself the same love and consideration that you would show a friend. Recall that everyone errs occasionally, and that's acceptable.

You establish the ideal conditions for inner clarity to arise by stilling the mind, practicing presence, and calming the inner critic. You can access your creativity, establish a connection with your intuition, and feel incredibly at peace and well-being in this quiet place.

Not only does this fresh perspective make one feel wonderful, but it also has practical applications. You may approach problems with clarity, make wise choices, and handle life's complications more easily when your mind is calm. You improve your ability to solve problems, be a more considerate friend, and take an active role in the world.

THE CHATTERBOX WITHIN

Imagine standing in a busy marketplace and attempting to hear a tiny whisper. It's similar to trying to use your inner wisdom or intuition when your head is racing with ideas. The subtle messages are drowned out by mental clutter, which makes it hard to be creative, handle problems well, or just take a moment to relax.

This mental chatter might appear in a number of ways:

- **The Worry Wart:** "What if I fail?" "Have I locked the door?" "How will people perceive me?" You can't be in the present moment because of your persistent fears, which keep you mired in the future.

- **The Overthinker:** You go over previous conversations again, evaluate every choice in great depth, and deconstruct every decision. You become immobilized and unable to act as a result of this rumination.

- **The To-Do Tyrant:** Your mind starts creating lists and deadlines without stopping. It is stressful and challenging to decompress and refuel under this continual pressure.

You can make room for inner insight to surface by stilling your mind. It's similar to lowering the radio's volume so you can hear more important but softer information. You may access your intuition, unleash your creativity, and feel deeply at peace and in good health with this newfound calm.

TAMING THE EGO

Everybody has an ego, which is the aspect of the psyche that yearns for dominance, approval, and a sense of superiority. It's the voice that mumbles things like, "I need to look well in front of others" or "I'm better than them." The ego can be a helpful tool, inspiring us to work hard and pursue success. However, an unbridled ego may also be a major cause of negativity in our lives.

This is how our ego misleads us:

- **The Comparison Trap**: Comparing ourselves to others is the ego's favorite activity. We become jealous and feel inadequate and insecure when we think someone is "better" than us. This never-ending comparison game is a surefire way to make yourself unhappy.

- **The Need for Control:** The ego aspires to be in charge of everything and everyone in our immediate environment. Since life rarely goes as planned, this drive for control frequently results in worry and annoyance.

- **Fear of Failure:** The ego despises looking bad. We might get immobilized by this dread of failing, which keeps us from taking chances or moving beyond our comfort zones. It prevents us from growing and keeps us mired in a self-doubt loop.

Quieting the Ego's Chatter

The good news is that you don't have to let your ego rule your life. Here are a few strategies to tame its harmful effects:

- **The key is self-awareness**. Identifying the voice of your ego is the first step. Take note of the feelings and ideas that result from comparison, control, or failure-related dread.
- **Shift Your Focus:** Consider your own journey, your special talents, and your personal development rather than comparing yourself to others. Enjoy every victory, no matter how tiny.
- **Accept Imperfection:** Give up the need for perfection in everything. Errors are unavoidable and frequently present our best teaching moments. Accept imperfection and put progress ahead of perfection.

- **Exercise Gratitude:** Taking the time to recognize and be grateful for all of life's blessings helps you become more content and helps you move away from selfish desires.

You can make room for a more genuine version of yourself to surface by quieting your ego's voice. You start to feel more connected to your own worth and less focused on getting approval from others. You have more empathy, humility, and a desire to keep learning and developing as you go through life. The cornerstone in becoming an Awakened Being is this inward transformation.

MEDITATION

Are you feeling too much mental noise? Your off-switch, or quick route to inner clarity, can be meditation. It's not about trying to reach some kind of zen state of mind. It's about training your attention to stay in the present moment and not let your anxieties and thoughts take over. To get you started, try this easy guided meditation:

Find Your Quiet Space: Turn down the lights, locate a peaceful area where you won't be bothered, and settle into a cozy chair or cushion. Sit up tall but not stiff. Imagine a gentle thread pulling the crown of your head towards the ceiling, lengthening your spine. Close your eyes gently, or soften your gaze If it's more comfortable for you,

Focus on Your Breath: Grasp your tummy with one hand and your chest with the other. Breathe slowly and deeply through your nose. With every breath in, feel your tummy sink, and with every breath out, feel it rise. Without attempting to force it, pay attention to the natural rhythm of your breathing. If your thoughts stray—which they will—gently bring them back to your breathing without passing judgment.

Body Scan: After spending a few minutes concentrating on your breathing, pause to look over your entire body. Wiggle your fingers and toes, beginning at your toes. Take note of any bodily feelings, such as warmth, coolness, tension, and relaxation. Gradually raise your awareness of your body, naming every area objectively.

Embracing Thoughts Like Clouds: Visualize your ideas as clouds floating across a wide blue sky when they arise, which they will. You just watch the clouds come and go; you don't cling to them. Maintain your focus on your breathing, and if your mind wanders, gently and compassionately bring it back to the present moment.

Bringing It All Together: Bring your attention back to your breathing for the last few minutes of your meditation. Experience the sensation of chilly air entering your nose and your chest rising and falling. Savor this peaceful moment and this area of inner clarity.

Gently Waking Up: Breathe deeply a few times and wriggle your fingers and toes again when you're ready to conclude your meditation. Open your eyes slowly and give yourself a chance to get your bearings. Avoid diving right back into your head chatter. Keep this feeling of presence and serenity with you all day.

Recall that practicing meditation is more important than doing it flawlessly. Even a short daily meditation session can make a big difference in your capacity to develop inner clarity and quiet the mind if you put in persistent effort. Thus, practice self-compassion, patience, and enjoy the journey.

DISCERNING YOUR INTUITION

Our intuition, that inner knowledge that nudges us in the correct direction and whispers guidance frequently gets drowns out by mental clutter. The good news is that you can develop your intuition and learn to trust its subtle suggestions with a little work.

To help you get started, consider these few exercises:

- **Dream Diary:** Dreams are a potent gateway to your subconscious, which is where intuition is typically found. As soon as you wake up, write down your dreams in the dream diary that you should keep by your bed. Make a note of your memories, even if they are simply snippets; they could be important hints. You may eventually begin to notice recurring themes or symbols that provide direction for your daily life.

- **Body Mapping:** Your body is a fount of intuitive knowledge. Locate a calm area, settle into a comfortable position, and shut your eyes. Breathe deeply for a few moments to help you center. Now start focusing your awareness on every area of your body, from head to toe, as you scan it. Take note of any hot spots, sore spots, or points of stress. These feelings may be your body's method of expressing itself to you. Before a big presentation, do you feel like you have a knot in your stomach? Maybe there's an underlying anxiety that your intuition is catching up on.

- **Gut Feeling Experiment:** Throughout the day, be mindful of those ephemeral "gut feelings"—a sudden suspicion or an unexplained want to act (or not act). Give these emotions some attention when they come up. Never write them off as unreasonable; they could be your intuition nudging you in the direction of important advice.

Try following your intuition the next time you have a gut feeling.

- **The "Notice and Reflect" Technique:** Throughout the day, stop for brief moments to observe your surroundings. What catches your attention among the sights, sounds, or smells? Are there any recurring themes or coincidental events? You can become more receptive to your intuition's gentle prods and nuzzles by learning to observe more.

Intuition isn't always a clear voice demanding answers. It could be a momentary sight, a hunch, or a faint emotion. The secret is to develop a calm feeling of awareness and to believe the nudges from your inner knowing. You'll discover that as you work through these exercises and develop your intuition, you're able to make more intuitive decisions, overcome obstacles more skillfully, and lead a genuine and satisfying life.

CHAPTER 4

DISCOVERING YOUR LIFE'S PURPOSE

Imagine a world in which each and every person awakens to a daily sense of purpose, a profound awareness of their purpose, and the special gifts they bring to the world. This is the possibility that everyone of us has as Awakened Beings; it is not a utopian dream.

Finding your life's meaning isn't about fulfilling some sort of predetermined fate. It's about directing your special abilities, interests, and moral principles toward something bigger than yourself. It all comes down to making a lasting impression on the world in a way that brings you joy and fulfillment.

However, how do we begin our search for purpose? Here are some effective techniques to help you:

Discovering Your Passion

What brings joy to your heart? Which activities cause you to lose track of time because they engross you so much? These interests are important indicators of your life's purpose. Here's how to reconnect with them:

- **Life Assessment:** Examine your life from a distance, taking into account your early aspirations, prior experiences, and present interests. What kinds of things made you happy and fulfilled?
- **Spark a Fire:** Don't be scared to try new things! Enroll in a course, lend a helping hand to a worthy cause, or discover new interests. You are more likely to find a secret passion that fuels your purpose if you immerse yourself in a variety of situations.

Identifying Your Strengths

Each of us has special abilities and capabilities that enable us to complete some jobs quickly and joyfully. Finding these strengths is essential to aligning your purpose to your mission. To locate yours, try these methods:

- **Evaluations of Strengths**: Numerous online tests are available to determine your greatest strengths. These tests can provide important insights into your innate abilities, even though they are not conclusive.

- **Opinions from Other People:** Find out what your mentors, coworkers, and reliable friends think are your strong points. What are your strongest tasks? What special contributions can you give to a group or a project?

- **Previous Achievements:** Think back to your previous successes. Which undertakings made you feel accomplished and satisfied? Which abilities did you use to your advantage to succeed? These prior encounters may provide important hints about your strong points.

Living by Your Values

Your life is guided by the essential principles that comprise your core values. These are the things that are deeply important to you and are not negotiable. It may be being creative, giving to others, or leading a sustainable existence. You can make sure that your efforts are not only profoundly rewarding but also have an impact by matching your mission with your values.

Here's how to revisit your core values:

- **Values in Action**: Look at those you find admirable. Which traits do they exhibit? It's likely that those attributes align with your own basic principles.
- **The "Would I?" Test:** When you happen to be faced with a decision, big or small, ask yourself, "Would this action align with my core values?" If the answer happens to be no, it might be leading you down a path that feels inauthentic.
- **Evolving Values:** Recall that your values are subject to change. Your values may change as

you develop and gain knowledge. Make sure your core values are still directing you toward a meaningful life by going over and improving them on a regular basis.

The Power of Purpose in Action

It's time to put your purpose into action after you've gotten a glimpse of it. Here are a few methods to get going:

- **Start Small:** Don't let the urge to make significant life adjustments overwhelm you. Start by adding modest daily activities to your schedule that are in line with your objective. Give your time to a cause you are passionate about, invest in learning a new skill, or just make decisions that align with your principles.
- **Find Your Tribe:** Those who motivate you to live your purpose and who share your beliefs should be in your immediate vicinity. Seek out mentors, become involved in communities, or work with people who are changing the world.

A life filled with meaning, fulfillment, and a profound sense of connection to something more than oneself is a life lived with purpose. You have the ability to use your special talents and purpose as an Awakened Being to alter the world for the better by starting a positive chain reaction.

BEYOND THE TO-DO LIST

To-do lists are essential to our society. We chase dreams, one achievement at a time, always looking forward to the next big thing. What if, however, there was a more satisfying way to live a life driven by purpose?

The truth is that having a purpose goes beyond simply crossing things off a list. It's about developing into a particular kind of person—someone who lives out their principles and offers the world their special talents. Not only the destination matters, but also the journey.

Without a doubt, goals can be helpful instruments for concentrating your efforts and reaching particular objectives. However, they can make you feel disoriented and empty if they take up all of your attention. Here's how to change the way you think:

- **From Doing to Being:** Consider "who" you want to become in the process rather than just "what" you need to do. What attributes does your objective require of you? Feelings of compassion? Originality? Adaptability? Develop these traits on a regular basis, and you'll see how your behaviors flow naturally from who you are.

- **The Joy of the Journey:** Instead of concentrating only on the outcome, appreciate the process of creation, the act of creating itself, and the present now. The destination becomes less of a pressure point and more of a natural unfolding when you discover joy in the process.

- **Openness to Flow:** Plans rarely work out in life. Accept the unanticipated detours and turns. Sometimes these side trips lead to the most meaningful discoveries. Despite the fact that it may not feel like it, have faith that you are precisely where you should be.

You can find greater motivation and fulfillment by changing your attention from accomplishing to embodying. Your purpose then becomes more about the kind of impact you want to make on the world, one moment at a time, than about reaching a particular goal. This is the fundamental aspect of leading a purpose-driven life that goes beyond a to-do list.

IDENTIFYING YOUR GIFTS AND TALENTS

Everybody has certain talents and gifts that are just waiting to be discovered. These gifts are the innate abilities that make you happy and enable you to make a significant contribution to the world; they are not only about fancy skills or awards.

Here's a little exercise to help you discover your special talents:

The Three Circles

Using a pen and paper, create three circles that overlap each other. Put "Strengths" in the first circle, "Passions" in the second, and "Values" in the third. Now brainstorm and put words or phrases that speak to you in each circle.

- **Strengths Circle:** What skills come easily to you? Which chores, albeit difficult for others, are easy for you? This can include anything from creative problem-solving to analytical thinking, from public speaking to handicrafts.

- **Passions Circle:** What brings you joy in your heart? Which activities cause you to lose track of time because they engross you so much? This could be anything from creating art to performing music, from lending a hand to volunteering in the outdoors.

- **Values Circle:** What principles guide your actions? Which values direct your life? This might be anything from creativity and sustainability to honesty and compassion.

Examine the sweet spot now that the circles overlap. This is the sweet spot where your values, interests, and strengths come together. Your special talents, the innate skills that make you happy and enable you to make a significant contribution to the world, are right here.

ALIGNING WITH YOUR DHARMA

Dharma. These days, this Sanskrit phrase is frequently used, but what does it actually mean? Your dharma is essentially your life's mission, but it goes deeper than that. It's a special place where your passions, skills, and the needs of the world converge. It's about making a good impact on the fabric of existence by applying your talents to a cause bigger than yourself.

Consider it this way: each of us is a different singer in the symphony of life. The melody, the core of your offering, is your mission. Your dharma, however, provides the harmony—the way your skills and interests mesh with the demands of the universe to produce something lovely and significant.

Your path toward your dharma is an evolving one; it has no set destination. Your abilities vary as you learn and develop, and the needs of the environment around you shift as well. Your dharma may change and evolve, but the fundamental principle—the desire to use your special talents to benefit others—never changes.

Here's how Dharma aligns with your purpose:

- **Uniqueness with Universality:** Unique to you, your Dharma is a reflection of your spirit. However, it also fulfills a more general function, enhancing the welfare of the entire population. Imagine an enormous curtain where every thread is distinct in hue and texture and is skillfully weaved to produce a breathtaking piece of artwork. Your dharma is the special thread that you provide to the greater fabric of life, giving it strength and beauty.

- **Beyond Action Alone**: Dharma is not only about action; it's also about how you do it. It's about bringing sincerity, empathy, and a feeling of service to what you do. Not only does the teacher impart knowledge, but they also foster a passion for studying. The physician is the one who cures spirits in addition to bodies.

- **The Joyful Path:** When you're living your Dharma, it doesn't feel like work. It seems like a joyous manifestation of your innermost aspirations to contribute, an expansion of who you are. Of course, there may be difficulties along the way, but ultimately, the experience is one of purpose and fulfillment.

Finding your preordained destiny is not the goal of discovering your Dharma. It's about the ongoing exploration of your passions, values, and talents. Your dharma will become more apparent as you deepen your comprehension of these fundamental facets of who you are, pointing you in the direction of a meaningful existence.

PUTTING PURPOSE INTO ACTION

You now have a glimpse of your life's purpose and know what it is that you are here to do. What happens next? Here's how to turn your idea into real action:

- **Vision Board:** Paint a picture of your purpose. Take out some magazines and a piece of cardboard, then let your imagination run wild. Cut out pictures, phrases, or anything else that helps you visualize your goal. Place them on the board to make a collage that represents your goals. You will remain inspired and goal-focused with the help of this visual reminder.

- **Small Steps, Big Impact:** Avoid being overwhelmed by the magnitude of altering your complete life in a single day. Begin modestly. Is it possible for you to donate one hour of your time each week to a cause that shares your values? Can you commit 30 minutes a day to learning a skill that will help you achieve your objectives? Over time, little, regular acts add up and guide you closer to your goal.

- **The "Just One Thing" Challenge:** Are you feeling overwhelmed? Utilizing the "Just One Thing" challenge to simplify your approach. "What's just one tiny action I can take today that resonates with my purpose?" should be your first morning question. It might be anything, such as reading a journal entry about your goals or contacting a possible mentor in your profession. Making progress is as simple as taking one tiny step every day.

- **Find Your Cheerleaders:** Keep yourself surrounded by encouraging and motivating individuals. This might be a friend, a mentor, or even an online group of people who share your interests. Having other people know your goal gives you a sense of accountability and keeps you inspired as you journey.

- **Celebrate Progress, Not Perfection:** There will be hiccups, disappointments, and periods of uncertainty in the journey. That's alright!

Celebrate every step forward you've taken, no matter how tiny. Recognize your accomplishments, no matter how tiny. This encouragement keeps you inspired and serves as a reminder of your progress.

The secret to turning your goal from a distant dream into a lived reality is to act. Instead of waiting for the "ideal" time, begin using what you already have, where you are. You are getting closer to leading a life driven by purpose with each step you take and each thing you commit to.

PART III

LIVING A DIVINELY
GUIDED LIFE

CHAPTER 5

EMBRACING
SURRENDER AND TRUST

The idea that having control is essential to succeed is widely held in our society. We work hard and hustle through life, believing that if we push hard enough, the universe will yield to our will. However, another truth—the truth of trust and surrender—emerges for the Awakened Being.

Surrender does not mean giving up or being docile. It's about recognizing your control's limitations and allowing life to flow through you. It's about realizing that there is a greater picture, or grand design, to the universe that is sometimes difficult to see. When you give up, you let go of the desire to influence the result and have faith that, despite how uncomfortable it may seem, you are right where you are supposed to be.

This is a difficult notion to understand at times. We've been indoctrinated to think that happiness is the result of unrelenting effort and that security is found in control. However, what if real happiness comes from letting go and having faith in life's natural course?

Let's look at some ways practicing surrender and trust can change your experience:

The Illusion of Control

Life is, by its very nature, unpredictable. Relationships end, jobs are lost, and unforeseen circumstances divert us from our path. Anxiety and irritation are surefire outcomes when one clings to control when faced with this inescapable uncertainty. You can release yourself from the never-ending battle and create space for new opportunities by accepting that life is constantly changing.

This little activity will help you understand the illusion of control.

- Close your eyes and clench your fists as tightly as you can. Hold for a minute.. Hold on for a moment. Take note of the strain and pain in your hands and arms. Now, gradually remove the tension by opening your hands and letting go of your grip. That feels so much better, ahhhh. Giving up control results in calm and relaxation, whereas clinging to control causes stress and discomfort.

Letting Go of Fear

Often, the greatest barrier to giving up is fear. We are afraid of what is outside our perceived control and the unknown. However, when we surrender, we make room for something bigger to happen—something we could never have orchestrated ourselves.

Here's how to address the fear that arises with surrender:

- **Confront Your Fears:** Rather than suppressing your fear, face it. Consider asking yourself,

"What do I fear?" Your dread becomes less powerful the moment you give it a name.

- **Trust the Process:** Remember that the universe is working in your favor, even when it seems like nothing is definite. This implies that, despite your inability to see it, a larger plan is developing.

The Power of Trust

Surrendering means developing a strong faith in how life will work out, not just letting things happen. It's about having faith that there's a greater purpose at work, even in the face of challenges. When you trust, you let go of the impulse to control every aspect of life and give yourself over to a power bigger than yourself.

Living with Surrender and Trust

So how can trust and surrender fit into daily life? Here are a few instances:

- **Relationships**: Give up trying to influence other people's behavior. Put your energy into communicating your own needs and truths, and have faith that the correct connections will arise on their own.

- **Career**: Try to match your skills and passion with a purpose that feels meaningful, rather than worrying too much about the little things. Have faith that when the stars align, the perfect opportunity will present itself.
- **Challenges**: When faced with challenges, see them as chances to improve. Have faith that everything happens for a reason, even if things go wrong.

Embracing trust and surrender does not imply passivity. It entails taking deliberate action that is in line with your goals and ideals and having faith that the universe will assist you on your path. Instead of being a strict controller, it's about learning to co-create with life.

You learn to move between effort and surrender as an Awakened Being. You act with inspiration and then have faith in the process. Knowing that the universe is on your side, you let go of the urge to exert control over the result. This method encourages resilience, inner serenity, and a profound understanding that you are on the right road and in the right place.

RELEASING CONTROL

The adage "You can't control everything" is well known. However, really understanding this idea and putting it into practice in our daily lives can be a humbling experience. We cling to control because it makes us feel secure and gives us the impression that we are the creators of our own happiness,

However, life is actually messy. It laughs at our well-constructed plans, turns on us, and throws curveballs. Anxiety and irritation are surefire outcomes when one clings to control when faced with this inescapable uncertainty. It is ultimately unsustainable and as tiring as trying to walk on a tightrope with bare hands.

How then do we let go of the reins? The solution is as follows:

- **Control is an Illusion**: On a beach, picture yourself attempting to control the waves with just your hands. Surely, it's a fruitless endeavor? The flow and rhythm of the water are unique. Life is like that ocean; it's a strong river with its own flow. Surrendering is not giving up; rather, it is realizing your lack of control and allowing life to unfold naturally around you.

Giving up control can be frightening. What if everything breaks down? What happens if we slip? Humans naturally react with terror to unknowns. The truth is, though, that maintaining power does not ensure security or contentment. Actually, it frequently results in the very outcomes we dread—missed chances, damaged bonds with others, and a persistent sense of unease.

Here's how to deal with the dread of giving up that comes with it:

- **Confront Your Fears:** Don't try to ignore your fear. Rather, accept it. Consider asking yourself, "What do I fear?" The more knowledge you have about your fear, the less control it will have over you.

- **Trust the Bigger Picture:** Remember that the cosmos is working in your favor even when things seem uncertain. Even when you can't see it, a big design is being revealed. Giving up control enables you to connect with this invisible force and allow a higher power to lead you.

Releasing control doesn't mean going passive; rather, it means letting go of the urge to plan every little thing. It's about having faith that you're not riding alone on this journey, even when you give up the reins. Along the journey, the universe is there to encourage you, point you in the correct path, and even surprise you with pleasant surprises.

TRUSTING THE DIVINE PLAN

It takes more than just accepting the way things are in life to truly surrender; it takes developing a strong faith in the divine plan, the unseen tide that leads you to your greatest good. This trust is a sense that there is a larger plan at work, even in the midst of chaos or unpredictability. It is not blind faith. The following actions can help to foster this trust:

- **Affirmations for Trust**: Words have influence. Repetition of uplifting statements can help rewire your brain and increase faith in God's purpose. Here are some useful examples:
"I have faith that everything exists to serve my best   interests."
"I accept life's flow and let go of my demand for control."
"Even though it seems uncertain, I am on the perfect path."

- **Visualization**: Shut your eyes and inhale deeply many times. Picture yourself perched on a bridge's brink. Your perfect existence, full of fulfillment, joy, and purpose, is waiting for you on the other side. The bridge itself is a symbol of the divine purpose coming to pass. It may lead you to your destination, but it may also contain curves, twists, and even some unstable parts.

Imagine yourself walking fearlessly onto the bridge and putting your faith in it to support you even in the face of uncertainty.

- **Gratitude as a Bridge to Trust**: A trusting heart is one that is appreciative. You change your viewpoint and develop faith in the wealth of the universe when you concentrate on the positive aspects of your life, no matter how minor. Every day, set aside some time to consider your blessings. Say "thank you" aloud for all the blessings in your life, or write them down in a journal.

- **Finding the Lessons in Challenges:** We are dealt curveballs in life. It is unavoidable. However, the same difficulties might present chances for development and change if they are seen through the prism of trust. What lesson is this situation attempting to teach me? ask yourself. "How can I grow stronger and more resilient from this experience?" Seeking the bright side of things helps you develop the confidence that everything happens for a reason, no matter how bad things get.

As with any muscle, trust grows stronger with use. The more you allow life to flow through you, the more you'll encounter synchronicities—meaningful coincidences that serve as subtle confirmations of God's purpose. By developing trust, you free yourself from the weight of control and make room for the abundance and happiness that come with following the path of surrender.

NAVIGATING CHALLENGES WITH GRACE

Not everything in life is sunshine and rainbows. There will be unanticipated turns, hiccups in the path, and times when everything will seem unclear to you. However, it is in these trying moments that the true power of surrender and trust truly show their strength.

Permit me to relate a personal tale: I had my sights set on a particular career path for years. I gave it everything I had, vividly picturing the future. The rug was then pulled out from under me one day. The chance I had been pursuing disappeared. When devastation struck, my first instinct was to fight, to force reality to comply with my wishes.

However, another voice could be heard in that place of hopelessness. It was a whisper, a quiet knowing, to trust the process. It wasn't easy to give in to the disappointment, but I gradually started to let go. I concentrated on my skills, my resiliency, and my optimistic outlook.

Here's the twist:: A few months later, something even greater came up—an opportunity I could never have orchestrated on my own. It aligned perfectly with my purpose and played to my strengths in ways I hadn't even imagined. I learned a valuable lesson from that experience: sometimes the universe has a better plan than we do.

Everyone has difficulties. It's important to approach them with grace rather than angrily. This is what that looks like:

- **Acknowledge Your Emotions**: Don't hold your emotions within. Give yourself permission to experience your disappointment, frustration, and fury. However, resist letting those feelings control you.

- **Focus on What You Can Control:** Although life can be unpredictable, you always have the power to choose how you will react. Pay attention to your behavior, attitude, and resilience.

- **See the Bigger Picture:** Take a step back and attempt to see the problem from a wider angle. Is there a hidden lesson here? An opportunity for growth?

- **Trust the Process:** Recall that the cosmos is working in your favor even when it seems like everything is crumbling. Trust that, even though you aren't able to see it yet, there's a bigger plan unfolding.

Turning obstacles into stepping stones is possible when you practice trust and surrender. You gain the ability to gracefully handle life's unexpected turns and come out stronger, wiser, and more receptive to the lovely way your journey plays out.

ALIGNING WITH DIVINE WILL

When considered through the prism of the divine, surrender and trust take on an entirely new meaning. Divine will isn't some outside power forcing its agenda upon you. It is the same spirit that permeates everything—the intelligence that directs the stars' and your heart's beat. You become a co-creator with the cosmos when you connect yourself with this flow through surrender and trust.

Imagine a magnificent river. You could decide to fight the current, exhausting yourself in the process. Alternately, you can learn how to navigate the rapids, and harness the force of the river to help you go forward. Embracing divine will is akin to allowing the river to carry you to your destination, knowing that in the end, it will guide you there.

Here are a few strategies for developing this alignment:

- **Intuition as Your Guide:** Your intuition is your inner compass, your gut instinct or hunch. It whispers instructions from the divine within. Calming your thoughts and developing your gut feelings makes you more sensitive to the gentle prods that point you in the direction of alignment.
- **Service to Others**: Serving others is one of the most effective methods to synchronize with the will of the divine. You become a channel for the love and compassion of the divine when you use your abilities to uplift those around you.
- **Living with Integrity:** You automatically align yourself with the innate goodness of the universe when you live a life that is consistent with your ideals and behave in an honest and compassionate manner.

Surrendering to divine will does not make you a blind passivity. It involves acting with inspiration, being true

to your purpose, and trusting that the universe will help
you along the way.

CHAPTER 6

MANIFESTING YOUR DREAMS WITH DIVINE CO-CREATION

We've all heard the tales of lottery winners, the overnight successes, and desires that appear to materialize magically. It's easy to write these tales off as coincidences or acts of pure chance. However, a deeper truth is at work for the Awakened Being: the truth of co-creation with the divine.

Manifesting your dreams is not about making the universe submit to your will. It's about bringing your desires to life in partnership with the divine by putting yourself in alignment with the creative flow of existence. In addition to taking action, this co-creation calls for an open mind to the unexpected and a willingness to trust how life will work out.

Here's how to become an active co-creator instead of just a passive wisher:

Clarity: The Foundation of Manifestation

To start realizing your dreams, you must have absolute clarity. What is it that you want specifically? What deeper needs, beyond the wants on the surface, are you hoping to meet?

Here are a few strategies for developing clarity:

- **Vision Board 2.0:** Go beyond the vision board you created in Chapter 4. Jot down all of your desires, including images, affirmations, and feelings. How will you feel when you realize this dream? How will it affect the environment around you, and how will it affect your life?

- **Journaling for Clarity:** Make time every day to write in your journal about your aspirations. Write freely and without inhibitions, letting your innermost thoughts come to the surface. Keep an eye out for reoccurring themes and feelings as you write. These can provide insightful information about your true intentions.

Alignment: Bringing Your Desires into Harmony

Alignment is the next step once your desires are clear. Do your dreams align with your life's purpose and your core values? If not, there may be internal strife, which could prevent manifestation.

This is a way to guarantee alignment:

- **Values Check**: Go over your basic beliefs again (Chapter 4). Do your core beliefs align with the outcome you want? If not, now might be a good moment to reconsider your goal or figure out how to get there in a way that is consistent with your moral principles.
- **Intuition as Your Guide**: Does your dream fill you with enthusiasm and anticipation? Or is there a persistent doubt or a sense of being untrue to yourself? Have faith in your instincts. Your ambitions may not be entirely in line with who

you truly are if anything seems strange in your gut.

Action: Taking Inspired Steps

While alignment and clarity are essential, inspired action is also necessary for manifestation. Passivity is not rewarded by the cosmos. It reacts to your vigor, your dedication, and your readiness to move forward.

This is how to put intention into action:

- **Small Steps, Big Impact:** Remain calm in the face of the immensity of your dreams. Start by making tiny, doable changes that get you closer to your objective. This momentum helps you stay focused on the manifestation process and boosts your confidence.

- **Inspired Action vs. Forceful Action:** There is a distinction between acting out of inspiration and forcing others into doing something. Inspired action has a carefree, almost lighthearted quality. When one uses force, it feels like they are fighting against resistance. Have faith in your instincts to lead you in the direction of motivated action that is in harmony with the universal flow.

Living the Awakened Life: Beyond Manifestation

While it's a useful tool, realizing your dreams isn't the ultimate aim of the Awakened Being. Living a life of connection, service, and purpose is what gives life its genuine meaning. You have a greater sense of fulfillment when you use your manifestations to better the world, yourself, and the people around you.

This is how a life of purpose and manifestation may coexist:

- **Manifesting for the Collective:** Don't only manifest in order to benefit yourself. Make the most of your desires to change the world for the better. Dream of methods to improve the planet for future generations, of inventions that advance humanity, and of answers to the world's problems.

- **Service as Manifestation:** The act of serving itself can occasionally be the greatest manifestation. Give to those in need by giving your time, talents, or just your kindness. Giving allows you to become more receptive to receiving.

The divine and the Awakened Being collaborate on creation. You are a strong force in the cosmos, with the ability to influence both your own reality and a world full of opportunities. Accept the power of manifestation, but exercise caution and keep the greater good, compassion, and service at the forefront of your actions. As you proceed, you'll find that the process of manifesting is just as transformative as the final destination.

CO-CREATING WITH THE UNIVERSE

Co-creation is not about barking orders at the universe or making it do what you want it to do. It's about your intentions and the guiding forces of the invisible cosmos working in perfect harmony. Intention and action are two essential components of co-creation.

Intention

Your intention serves as a compass to direct you to your intended location. Here's how to make your intention clear:

- **Know Your Why:** Clarify the "why" of your desires in addition to the "what." Which deeper desires or ideals will this dream fulfill if it comes true?
- **Specificity is Key**: Wishing for "more money" is not enough. Describe your definition of "more money" and how it will make your life better. Your co-creation with the cosmos becomes more focused the clearer your intention is.

Action

Merely having intentions won't get you there. In order to move forward, you must act. How to convert intention into motivated action is as follows:

- **Aligned Action:** Not every action is taken equally. Take actions that are consistent with your purpose and values. Inspired activity feels light and effortless, like catching the wind in your sails, whereas forceful action feels like pushing against something.

- **Small Steps, Big Impact:** Avoid becoming intimidated by the ocean's size. Begin with manageable, tiny steps that get you closer to your objective. Regular, motivated actions create momentum and keep you involved in the co-creation process. Consistency is essential.

The universe reacts. You allow the process of co-creation to flow through you when you have a clear intention and follow your inspiration. The cosmos may open your eyes to new possibilities, guide you in new ways, or put supportive individuals in your path. Keep an open mind to these options and have faith that the journey is going just as it should.

THE POWER OF GRATITUDE

The key component that unlocks the full potential of your co-creation process is gratitude. You send a strong message to the universe when you show gratitude for all of the blessings in your life, no matter how small: "I appreciate what I have, and I'm open to getting more."

Consider it this way: being grateful opens up your energetic field, making room for abundance to enter. You keep yourself from experiencing the very things you want when your attention is always on what you don't have. Experiencing gratitude allows you to see the infinite possibilities of the cosmos.

OVERCOMING RESISTANCE

You've recognized your goals, connected them to your purpose, and moved inspiredly to take action. However, something doesn't feel quite right. It's possible that you are facing resistance—that inner force that raises obstacles and whispers doubts. Resistance can be cunning, appearing as fear, procrastination, or self-defeating thoughts. Don't give up, though! This is how you recognize opposition and go past it so that your manifestation magic never stops.

Recognizing the Signs

Recognizing resistance when it manifests itself is the first step. Here are a few typical indicators:

- **Procrastination Paralysis:** You come up with a gazillion reasons not to move toward your goals.
- **The Inner Critic:** You hear a voice in your head telling you that you're not good enough or that you can't do what you set out to do.
- **Overthinking and Analysis:** You become mired in the planning stage, scrutinizing every aspect nonstop and never making the initial move.

Facing Your Fears

It's time to address resistance head-on once you've discovered it. Consider this:

- What fear do I have? Is there a fear of failing? Fear of being successful? By giving your fear a name, you can lessen its influence.
- Does this fear help me? Is it preventing me from growing or advancing? Fear often tells us that we're headed in the right direction, but it also forces us to step outside of our comfort zone.

Changing the Way You Think

Unfavorable self-talk is a common source of resistance. This is how to reinterpret those constricting thoughts:

- "I'm learning" replaces "I can't." Focus on your development and your openness to picking up new skills.
- "I'm not good enough" transforms into "I deserve to realize my potential." Have faith in your own abilities to bring about the things you want.

LIVING WITH ABUNDANCE

Abundance isn't just about attracting fancy cars and material possessions. It's a mindset, a profound understanding that goodness abounds in the universe and that you are deserving of it. It's about appreciating the abundance and gifts that are already in your life, which you frequently take for granted.

Here's a perspective shift to help you create an abundant life:

- **Reframing Scarcity:** We tend to focus on what is absent rather than what is there since our brains are biased toward negativity. Dispute this idea of scarcity. Reframe the thought to be, "I have enough time for what is genuinely important today," as opposed to, "I don't have enough time."

- **Abundance is Everywhere:** Look about you. Observe the kindness of strangers, the beauty of the natural world, and the laughter of children. There is abundance everywhere, just waiting to be recognized. By practicing this awareness, you make room for more positive things to come into your life.

- **Celebrate the Small Wins:** Don't wait for enormous successes to acknowledge and appreciate your riches. Appreciate the little things in life, like a job well done, a nice word spoken, or a quiet time. Appreciating these tiny victories helps you feel abundant in life.

Abundance-driven living isn't about excess or greed. It's about believing that the universe works in harmony to provide for your needs and recognizing the gifts you already have in life. It's about being receptive to love, joy, creativity, and all the positive things in life, not just monetary possessions.

PART IV

INTEGRATION AND BEYOND

CHAPTER 7

SUSTAINING YOUR AWAKENED LIFE

Awakening is a lifelong process rather than an isolated occurrence. There will be mountaintop moments of clarity and blissful connection, but there will also be troughs of uncertainty, annoyance, and even a brief waning of your heightened consciousness. This entire process is a part of it.

Cultivating practices that nourish your spirit, keep you grounded, and enable you to weather life's inevitable storms is , in key to maintaining an awakened existence. Here are some vital resources for your road toward awakening:

Daily Activities to Lead an Awakened Life

- **Meditation:** The foundation of an awakened existence is meditation. It's a method for calming the mind, developing inner harmony, and making a deeper connection to who you are. Choose a meditation method that feels right for you among the many available. Daily meditation, even for only a few minutes, can have a significant impact.

- **Mindfulness**: The discipline of being mindful involves focusing attention on the here and now without passing judgment. It involves becoming conscious of your feelings, ideas, and bodily experiences. By keeping you rooted in the here and now, mindfulness helps you avoid being carried away by negativity or lost in concerns about the future.

- **Gratitude Practice:** Gratitude is a great technique for developing abundance and changing your attitude, as we covered in Chapter 6. Every day, set aside some time to consider all of the things for which you are thankful. Maintaining a thankfulness diary might be beneficial.

- **Link with Nature:** Spending time in nature is a powerful way to re-establish your connection to your true self and revitalize your soul. Take some time to spend outside, whether it's by taking a stroll around the park, hiking through the forest, or just relaxing in your backyard. Inhale the clean air, feel the sun on your face, and establish a connection with the environment.

- **Movement for the Body and Mind:** Physical and mental health depend on moving your body. Choose a hobby or pastime that you enjoy, whether it be stretching, yoga, dancing, or running. Exercise improves your mood, eases tension, and helps you focus better.

Facing Challenges with Awareness

There are obstacles for even the most Awakened Beings. Difficult feelings are unavoidable, as life can throw curveballs. The secret is to confront these difficulties with understanding and compassion rather than avoiding them.

Here are some strategies to get through challenging times:

- **Acknowledge Your Emotions:** Whether they be sadness, rage, or irritation, don't repress your feelings. Let them all out on you without passing judgment. With time, your emotions will become less powerful over you if you observe them objectively.

- **Practice Self-Compassion:** Treat yourself with kindness, particularly when things are difficult. You should have the same empathy and understanding for yourself as you would for a loved one.

- **Seek Support:** It is not our place to travel this route alone. Create a network of like-minded people who can support and guide you because they understand your journey. This could be a friend who offers assistance or a spiritual mentor.

Maintaining Your Connection to the Divine

Regardless of how you define it, maintaining your connection to the divine is crucial to living an awakened life. This relationship has the potential to be a great source of support, wisdom, and love.

Here are some strategies to maintain this relationship:

- **Take Some Time for Silent Thought:** Set aside some time every day to just be still and aware. This could be accomplished by meditation, prayer, or just spending some quiet time in nature. Give yourself permission to commune with quiet, which is the origin of all creation.

- **Pay Attention to Your Intuition:** This inner sense of direction comes from the divine inside and serves as your inner compass. Be mindful of your intuition, your hunches, and the subliminal cues that emanate from your inner knowledge.

- **Lead a Life of Service:** Serving others is one of the most effective methods to establish a spiritual connection. Make the most of your abilities and skills to improve the lives of those around you, support a cause that matters to you, and change the world.

Remember, You Are Not Alone

There will be times during your waking journey when you feel lost, alone, or unclear on where to go. Recall that you are traveling this route alongside a wide network of other awakened souls.

Here's how to foster a feeling of interconnectedness:

- Locate communities of Awakened Beings who share your values and goals. As you journey, surround yourself with uplifting people who will encourage and support you.
- Provide Assistance to Others: As you advance on your journey, don't be afraid to assist those who are awakening. One of the most effective ways to inspire and connect with others is to share your knowledge and experiences.

The Journey Continues

The journey of an Awakened Being is a never-ending process of development, learning, and metamorphosis. Accept the difficulties, acknowledge your accomplishments, and have faith in how your journey will play out.

Here are a few final points to remember:

- Growth is not linear, so if you encounter obstacles or periods of regression, don't give up. The process of awakening is not linear. You will experience moments of extreme alignment and connection, as well as moments of disorientation or disconnection. It's all just a part of the adventure. Have faith that everything happens for your benefit, including the obstacles.

- **Accept the Mystery:** One of life's greatest qualities is that it is full of mystery. Avoid becoming consumed by the need to own all the answers or to know everything. Even when you can't see the big picture, embrace the unknown, be open to new possibilities, and have faith that everything is working out properly in the cosmos.

- **Savor the Journey:** Life is an invaluable present that offers the chance to encounter the entire range of human feelings and establish a connection with the splendor of the surroundings. Avoid losing sight of the path in favor of the destination. Cheers to tiny and large achievements, embrace challenges, and savor the present now.

You have the ability to significantly alter the world for the better as an Awakened Being. You serve as a lighthouse and a link between the visible and invisible worlds. You transform yourself and help bring mankind closer to its collective awakening by tending to your enlightened existence. So set out on your amazing trip, shine brightly, and never stop.

INTEGRATING SPIRITUALITY INTO DAILY LIFE

It is not necessary to make significant life adjustments or go to a hilltop to live a spiritual life. It's about incorporating tiny rituals that uplift your soul and help you stay a part of something greater than yourself into your everyday routine. Here are a few simple integration tips:

- **Morning Ritual:** Make intention-setting a part of your morning routine. Think for a few quiet moments about the qualities you wish to develop that day: thankfulness, concentration, and serenity. Your intention might be written down, repeated aloud as a mantra, or just kept in your thoughts.

- **Mindful Moments:** Try incorporating little meditations throughout your day. While standing in line, take a few deep breaths, enjoy the flavor of your meal, or pay close attention to the sounds around you when you're out on a walk. These little mindfulness exercises help you stay grounded and in the present.

- **Appreciation Breaks:** Before you start eating, pause to recognize the people who cultivated the food, the laborers who prepared it, and the sustenance it offers. This practice elevates the mundane to a divine level and fosters gratitude.

- **Evening Reflection:** Consider your day for a little while before going to bed. For what do you feel thankful? Which obstacles did you successfully overcome? What knowledge did you gain? By doing this, you can develop self-awareness and carry over your daily insights into the following day.

Maintaining consistency is essential. Regularly engaging in even modest activities can make a big difference in your life. Don't get overwhelmed by the idea of grand rituals; instead, incorporate these easy rituals into your daily routine and observe how a sense of the sacred permeates your existence.

MAINTAINING BALANCE

The following advice can help you stay balanced:

- **Plan Your Practices:** Handle your spiritual activities as though they were crucial appointments. Schedule time on your calendar for journaling, meditation, or outdoor activities. Achieving the desired results requires consistency.

- **Short Bursts of Inspiration:** You may maintain your connection without spending hours in meditation. Throughout the day, brief mindfulness meditation sessions might be as beneficial. Before a crucial meeting, take a few deep breaths, enjoy your coffee slowly in the morning, or play your favorite relaxing song while driving.

- **Infuse the Mundane:** Seek ways to bring a bit of the awakened perspective into your everyday routines. Take a purposeful approach to your work, develop compassionate relationships with coworkers, or see even the most routine tasks as chances to practice mindfulness.

- Pay attention to your body and mind. Avoid pushing yourself to the brink of exhaustion. Take a break from your spiritual activities and concentrate on grounding yourself if you're feeling overwhelmed. Never forget that everything else depends on your wellbeing.

BUILDING A SPIRITUAL COMMUNITY

All of us yearn for connection, particularly throughout this awakening process. Connecting with like-minded people and sharing your experiences, obstacles, and successes can be a really motivating and supportive community. This is how you locate your spiritual group:

- **Look for Online Communities:** There are many online communities devoted to spiritual awakening and progress on the internet. Look through forums, social media groups, and websites that share your interests.

- **Attend Workshops and Events:** Workshops, retreats, and other events are hosted by a number of spiritual leaders and groups. Meeting other enlightened beings and learning from enlightening masters might occur at these gatherings, which you should definitely attend.

- Sometimes, you are closer to your tribe than you realize. Keep your eyes and heart open. Stay open-minded while going about your everyday business. At the dog park, the coffee shop, or the yoga studio, you might run across someone who understands you. Have faith that, when you're willing, connections will come naturally.

It might also be quite beneficial to find a mentor. A mentor is a knowledgeable and experienced advisor who can help you on your path to awakening by providing advice, inspiration, and support.

These pointers will help you locate a mentor:

- **Seek Alignment:** Look for a mentor whose principles and teachings line up with your gut feelings. It is advisable to conduct interviews with several possible mentors before selecting one who seems like a good fit.

- **Trust Your Intuition:** Your intuition is the most crucial component. Does this individual motivate you? Do you perceive respect and trust from others? Consider your instincts while selecting a mentor.

- **Look for authenticity:** Steer clear of charismatic leaders and those who insist on unquestioning submission. You can discover your own truth and follow your own path with the help of a genuine mentor.

The process of creating a spiritual community is not easy. Remain calm, maintain an open heart, and have faith that the appropriate connections will materialize at the ideal moment. Your tribe's support and sense of belonging will be a tremendous force in your awakening process.

THE ONGOING JOURNEY

The Awakened Being's path is an adventure rather than a final destination. It's an ongoing process of growth, discovery, and transformation that lasts a lifetime. There will be valleys of uncertainty, irritation, and the sporadic sense of being lost, as well as moments of spectacular clarity and blissful connection at the peak of the mountain. Embrace it all.

This path is about living in the now, about meeting each day with an open heart and a mind eager to learn. It's about letting go of the urge for control and having faith in life as it happens, even when it doesn't feel definite. Recall that the most valuable lessons frequently come from the unanticipated turns and difficulties we encounter.

Remember these basic lessons as you proceed: enjoy the journey, accept the mystery, and realize that growth isn't linear. Never give up on education, never stop asking questions, and never stop stoking your inner spark of awareness.

This is your ongoing journey, a magnificent exploration of your potential as an Awakened Being. With each step you take, with each lesson learned, you contribute to your own transformation and the collective awakening of the world. So go forth, keep your light shining brightly, and remember – the adventure continues.

CONCLUSION

The journey of an Awakened Being is about continuous development, letting go of limiting ideas, and realizing your own potential rather than arriving at a predetermined place. This book has been a guide, providing techniques and resources to support your awakened existence. The true journey, though, starts now as you apply these realizations to your day-to-day activities.

Achieving an unending state of happiness is not the goal of living an awakened life. It's about accepting all aspects of the human experience, including happiness, grief, light, and shadow. It's about developing the grace, resiliency, and acute awareness necessary to overcome the inescapable obstacles.

There will be periods of uncertainty and unclear direction. It's alright. Uncertainty is a normal aspect of awakening. It can push you to learn more, challenge your presumptions, and eventually strengthen your foundation.

Remember that the universe is a huge and mysterious place. The beauty lies in the possibility that we will never know all the answers. Accept the unknown. Permit yourself to be taken aback by the unexpected twists and turns on your path. It is curiosity that fuels an awakened life, not certainty.

You and the universe become co-creators as Awakened Beings. You are now an active participant in the magnificent unfolding of reality, rather than just a passive spectator. Make contributions to the world around you with your newly awakened awareness. Raise up people in need, let your compassion be a lighthouse, and encourage others to discover their own inner strength.

Awakened existence is about helping mankind awaken as a whole, not about pursuing self-interest. The planet itself changes, and the collective consciousness moves as more and more people come to awareness. You are a vital part of this movement!

Here are some guiding ideas to keep in mind as you proceed:

Embrace the Mystery

The universe is a huge and amazing place that is full of mysteries and unknowns. Avoid being obsessed with controlling the result or needing to know all the answers. The mystery and the unfolding that are outside the purview of our limited comprehension are part of what makes life so beautiful. Accept the unknown with awe and be open to being taken aback by the coincidences and miracles life delivers.

Live with an Open Heart

A compassionate heart that exudes love and understanding for both oneself and other people is an awakened heart. Let go of preconceived notions and grudges, and develop compassion for the whole range of complexity that is the human experience. Your heart will open, and you will feel a sense of oneness that surpasses separation and a closer connection to all beings.

Be a Force for Positive Change

Awakening is a call to action, not a self-serving endeavor. Develop your inner light and use it to brighten the environment around you. Look for ways to make the world a more equitable, peaceful, and sustainable place. This could be achieved through charitable deeds, artistic pursuits, or just by showing kindness and compassion in all of your encounters.

Live Fully in the Present Moment

The future is unclear, and the past is gone. This is the only moment you really have. Develop mindfulness, the skill of being attentive and in the moment. Savor life's small pleasures, the splendor of the natural world, and the comfort of human connection. Avoid being engrossed in thoughts and worries about the past or the future. Because now is where life really happens, live life to the fullest in the present.

Trust the Journey

There will be moments when you doubt your direction, when uncertainty seeps in, and when it seems impossible to move forward. Have faith in life's course during these times. Don't forget that even when you can't see it, the cosmos has a big design. Give up trying to influence the result and accept what happens with an open mind and a trusting heart.

The Awakened Being is a continuously evolving soul that is dedicated to development, service, and leading a life that is filled with meaning and purpose rather than being a flawless saint. As you proceed on your trip, keep these words in mind:

- **You are worthy.** You deserve to live a happy, abundant, and loving life.
- **You are powerful.** You possess the ability to bring about constructive transformation in both your surroundings and yourself.

- **You are connected.** On this journey, you are not by yourself. Every one of us is entangled in a massive web of interconnectedness.

Thus, Awakened Being, go forth and radiate your light brightly. Accept the constant process of change, the mystery of life as it is revealed, and the profound joy of being awake. The world needs your unique gifts, your awakened heart, and your unwavering spirit.

To My Dearest Readers,

From the depths of my heart, thank you for embarking on this journey of awakening with me in "The Awakened Being: Living with Clarity, Purpose, and Divine Insight."

Your decision to explore these pages is a testament to your own desire to cultivate a life filled with clarity, purpose, and connection. I am honored to be a part of your growth and transformation.

As a small token of my appreciation, I have a special gift waiting for you! Head over to the QR code below to claim your gift and delve deeper into the wisdom explored in the book.

Leaving a review on Amazon is not only incredibly helpful for me as an author, but it also helps guide others who are seeking a path to awakening. Your honest feedback allows the message of "The Awakened

Being" to reach a wider audience and empower more individuals to live their most fulfilling lives.

Thank you again for being a part of this journey. May you continue to experience clarity, purpose, and divine insight on your path forward.

With gratitude,

Debra T. White

P.S. Don't forget to claim your special gift at the QR code below.

KINDLY SCAN THIS
CODE TO GET YOUR
GIFT

Made in the USA
Monee, IL
21 March 2025

14350817R00069